MARY JEAN CHAN

Flèche

T0272776

ff
FABER & FABER

First published in 2019
by Faber & Faber Ltd
The Bindery
51 Hatton Garden
London ECIN 8HN

Typeset by Hamish Ironside
Printed in England by TJ Books Limited, Padstow, Cornwall

A CIP record for this book is available from the British Library

ISBN 978-0-571-34804-6

Printed and bound in the UK on FSC® certified paper in line with our continuing
commitment to ethical business practices, sustainability and the environment.
For further information see faber.co.uk/environmental-policy

for my family

Preface

1. *We are defined against something, by what we are not and will never be.*

2. *Who will read this slim volume of mine, and with what preconceptions?*

3. *A poet I admire once told a British audience: we must call out monolingualism, since the world has forever been multilingual.*

4. *There are many reasons for my writing in your language. Ask your government, ask mine.* *

5. *This is a book of love poems.*

*Cf. The 1842 Treaty of Nanjing, the 1860 Convention of Beijing and the 1898 Convention for the Extension of Hong Kong Territory following British military aggression towards the Qing government during the First and Second Opium Wars.

Contents

CORPS-À-CORPS

Love takes off the masks that we fear we cannot live without and know we cannot live within.

JAMES BALDWIN

母
親
的
故
事

My Mother's Fables

Fairy Tales

I grew up with Aesop's Fables of the more sinister kind, in which a child would be forced to line up behind other children to slap their teacher in the face as a young Red Guard stood by, watching. Those adolescents were crazed colts: their hands a stampede, their mouths deep trenches of bone.

In Love and in War

There was a boy who loved my mother so much he hid his steamed bun in the haystack, told her to eat while he did her share of hard labour, urged sleep when the sun hung high at noon. She called him *Pumpkin* since she missed the gourd's reassuring weight, the land as starved as she was.

Red Night

Animals crowded the bathtub, which became God's ark, the night the flood came. The Guards took everything deemed *bourgeois*: a ceramic teapot, a mechanical watch, and my grandfather, who refused to be saved. My grandmother believed in God, so she forgave their fists, called them *sons*.

My Grandfather's Heart

A beating thing. A delicate muscle stops its cyclical motion, crushed by too much terror. He was only admitted to the workers' hospital after a former employee lied, claimed him as one of their own. An eleven-year-old sprints towards her father in this blood-lit *mise en scène*: a scripted tragedy.

That Child is My Mother

Listen: there is no measure for the tempo of grief. My mother would raid the fridge at midnight for a salted egg, some pickled carrots. I didn't know we were safe in a different city, a different year. Once, during a bedtime storytelling, she sobbed until I cried for help, but father was asleep.

Wet Nurse

for the woman who raised my mother

Shanghai, 1953

The milk pours from my body into
a strange mouth. It is always hungry
and so am I. The Yulan magnolias
are rioting in the back garden, unruly
children bored with yet another spring.
The mouth frees my nipple and leaks
tributaries down my skin. It has been
ninety-seven days since the city stole
my flesh. My husband and I have not
spoken since. He shall never touch me
again. When the mother goes to preach
the gospel, I pretend I am her, holding

my own daughter, promising to never
let go. The baby sees no problem with
two mothers. The father adores her at
a distance. Sixth child, third daughter,
beloved one. Some nights, I long for
a landslide in the mind, so I might bury
the moment I abandoned my daughter
at the station the morning of her birth,
weak from blood loss and fearful that a
wet nurse with child will never find work.
Now, when the baby smiles up at me,
another brushes my breast with its lips.

母親的故事

PARRY

Always

Do you ever write about me?
Mother, what do you think?
You are always where I begin.
Always the child who wanted to be
a boy, so you could be spared
by your mother-in-law.
Always the ear that hears you
translating my poems
with a bilingual dictionary.
Always the pen dreaming
it could redeem the years
you fled from, those
Red-Guarded days
and nightmares. Always
the mind's eye tracing
your frantic footsteps
towards the grandfather
I would never meet.
Always the lips wishing
they could kiss those mouths
you would approve of.

Dress

The same uniform for twelve years. A white skirt, blue collar, blue belt, blue hem. A dark, no-nonsense kind of blue. White as snowfall in Eden. You washed it every single day, made sure you ate in small bites, always wore an extra pad so none of the blood could seep through. You began wearing that dress at the age of six, your skin haunted by the British flag, so you could be *Chinese with English characteristics*. Each time you wore it, you shut your body up. Some girls wore theirs short, discoloured, tight. Head Girl, you reported them to the Office of the Headmistress for inappropriate behaviour, kept your dress at just the right length. Most mornings you see the face of a boy in the mirror. You expect to fall in love with him. Meanwhile, your fingers brush the wrist of another girl as you jostle into the assembly hall, and you understand that sin was never meant to be easy, only sweet. What memory might light up the pond you sat beside in dreams, eyeing so much depth it would be years before you dared? What curvature of tongue might you taste, as if another's breath were blessing? One night, you find yourself kneeling beside the pond. You dream. A voice says: *Hell is not other people.* You slip into the blue water, stripped of the glowing dress you wore for thousands of days.

Practice

As a teenager, fencing was the closest thing
I knew to desire, all the girls swapping one

>
> uniform for another before practice, their white
> dresses replaced by breeches. I thought we were

princes in a fairy tale with a twist, since
there were no princesses to be taken, wed.

>
> As knights, we were told to aim for an imaginary
> spot just above our opponent's left breast. Often,

I left a bruise: the blade's tip ricocheting off chest-
guards onto skin. Just as often, I would feel yellow

>
> blooms of ache where the girl I thought was beautiful
> had pierced my heart. Hours later, I would transform.

I would head back home with a deepening
sense of dread, my bruises fading to quiet.

A Hurry of English

What isn't obvious isn't obvious because I intend to obfuscate. O chews its own tail like a rabid dog. What does it say about me, this obsession written in a language I never chose? My desires dressed themselves in a hurry of English to avoid my mother's gaze. How I typed 'Shakespeare', then 'homoeroticism + Shakespeare' into Google, over and over. My mother did not understand the difference between English words, so she let me be. A public history seeps into the body, the way tea leaves soak up the scent of a fridge. An odourless room is not necessarily without trauma. We must interrogate the walls. My skin is yellow because it must. Love is kind because it must. Admit it, aloud.

Rules for a Chinese Child Buying Stationery
in a London Bookshop

Speak to the white
elderly man at the counter.
There will be many

more of them
in your life, but start
with him. Recall those syllables

you've whispered over and
over like some version
of the Lord's Prayer:

Our Father who art
in heaven and is
white and beyond skin.

Enunciate. He must hear
what you have to say
if you are to be helped.

Begin with *please*. Say
may I. End with *thank you*.
He will be delighted

to know you are polite,
soft-spoken, well-mannered.
You will be overjoyed

at his acceptance, a palm
reaching towards you
for something you are able to give.

You must hand over the money
quickly, but not in haste.
Your parents' wisdom comes

from *having had more salt*
than you have eaten rice.
This proverb is untranslatable,

but memorise and trust
in it all the same.
You are a tiny machine

being oiled
for the day you must
face the world,

a lifetime ahead of you,
years of salt
and rice and tea.

Magnolias

Picture a girl and a dinner table. The girl
will wait till she is told that she can sit at
the last seat available, after the men and

the boys, after the elderly. She does not
think it wrong, this box step of worries
she has learnt since she was old enough

to kneel beneath her mother's shadow
whenever she lost her cool. When the
girl was eight, she wanted to be a boy.

A storm of dresses fell from her mother's
lips. The sky was the colour of whitened
knuckles. The girl acquiesced, marooned

on her bed, mannequin beauty ready to
drown. Hours later, the girl dreams that
the dinner table is an ark she has finally

abandoned. The girl dreams that the words
sprouting like weeds from her mouth are not
weeds, but magnolias: her mother's favourite.

Flesh

Some days I watched shrimp and prawns
suffer: their deaths brutal, yet profoundly

ordinary – the crisp snip-snip of scissors
through vein after vein, the ripped shells

revealing pale grey flesh. Mother would
season the wounds with garlands of garlic,

ginger and lemongrass; turning up the heat
till the air itself became tinged with an oily

fragrance. I never refused the lightly charred
flesh, my tongue glad the way all beasts are

when allowed to eat their fill. Mother would
always have too much, her rice bowl emptying

so quickly I would never forget the three years
she became vegetarian: the famine leaving all

the trees bereft of their bark, the villagers so
grateful for something, anything, to chew on.

To the Grandmother Who Mistook Me for a Boy

I had my fist in your mouth – the day
you nearly died. Minutes into our meal
on Sunday, you slumped over and lay
so still we thought you'd left us to deal
with the grief you believed we deserved.
To curse our bodies for denying us rare
gifts of sons, despite offerings reserved
for deities disdainful of another prayer.
I wanted you to love me since mother
gave a damn about what you thought
of her; because among his brothers,
father was your favourite. So I fought
to keep you from biting your tongue: my
fist in your mouth, your love for me a lie.

Safe Space (1)

The closet is a space I climb into for comfort.
I nestle into the folds of my mother's dress, feel
the smooth silk of my father's tie on my cheek.
There is someone banging on the door. I know
she is still there, begging. I tell her to leave me
alone, let me be this frightened and lonely.
At least we will wake tomorrow and be a
family, seated at the table, my mother ladling
out Shanghainese pork knuckle, my father
slicing up salted duck with a surgical expertise

Conversation with Fantasy Mother

Dear fantasy mother, thank you
for taking my coming out as calmly
as a pond accepts a stone
flung into its depths.

You sieved my tears, added
an egg, then baked a beautiful cake.
You said: *Let us celebrate, for today*
you are reborn as my beloved.

The candles gleamed and the icing
was almost true – impossibly white –
coated with the sweetness of
sprinkles. We sat together

at the table and ate. Afterwards,
I returned to my room and touched
all the forbidden parts of myself, felt
a kindness I had not known in years.

A Wild Patience Has Taken Me This Far

I am writing in the voice of my most hopeful self

Amnesia was my daily bread

Thank God for fanfiction, for *It Gets Better*, for poets audacious enough to mention the body

Do you know what camouflage looks like on a day-to-day basis?

Checking the coast is clear before opening a single tab (and multiple decoys) on a screen

Surreptitiously reading Shakespeare (the scene where Cesario woos Olivia)

Watching my parents' faces for a sign to hold a tidal wave back

A daily prayer for the strength to confess nothing at all times

One day, it becomes a choice: to walk out of this life, or to begin living mine

I left half of my language behind to escape my impeccable persona

How I wanted to perform a heroic act to gain acceptance into the kingdom of ordinary people

To love a city and to not have it love you back is its own form of torture

When I met a beautiful stranger for the first time, I was deeply afraid of her tenderness

An appointment with a therapist led to a second date (I was given permission, needed permission)

She held my hand till I began to comprehend the territory of skin, its frantic heart and silent ponds

Most nights, I dream of my mother's face, by turns harsh and tender

In a nightmare, I shouted at her: *Neither you nor I are the enemy!*

What do mothers ask their own daughters, everywhere in the world?

Is there a question? Ask me something

the five stages

denial

when you ask me over & over how I knew // how do you *know*, with certainty // how *do* you know // what tells you this is love // rather than friendship or affection // or something else (anything else please . . .) // it was summer & I knew // the moment she walked into the room // how I wanted to be close & yet closer // to this stranger // who gestured for me to come closer // till I couldn't bear our proximity // in the shower // I touched the soapsuds // that clung to my face like heritage // having answered the question // I had been asking all my life // I couldn't stomach // the joy of it

anger

an innocent question: how did *you* know // you were in love with father // you said: but they are not the same thing // how dare you compare // your situation with ours // that summer // I knew with a certainty // that made my joints ache // with anger // the body rejecting // its own tragic needs // & wants // the urge to tear something apart // became apparent // I flung a pen & a stapler // across the room // & cried // she left me alone // I asked her to leave // me be // my tongue now a stranger in the mouth // *come back* // I wanted to shout // but my throat refused // to join the mutiny

bargaining

one night, the girl – a stranger // no longer – // whispers: *I could die happy right now* // she reaches over & our bodies // curl into one another // there is a knock // at the door // my heart is a stampede // she slips out of my arms & calls // to our flatmates: *hey,* // *what's up? we were just* // *watching a film* // she climbs back onto // her upper bunk // says *goodnight* // I lie down bereft // the ladder to the upper bunk taunts me // outside I find myself // caught in rain // body in ruins // when dawn comes // our eyes are full of confusion & thirst // she leans over // says nothing // I want to scream

depression

I am sitting in my friend's room // her smile is in the shape of a question // *have you ever wondered if you might like women* // I stare back at her // willing composure // a pathetic Juliet // her room is suddenly // a balcony // I wish I could leap from // the phone rings // I pick up // the sound of my mother's voice // she asks about the weather // in America // if I am cold // I am cold // stranded in the greying cold // I will silence upon unspeakable truths // *yes* // *mother* // *I am well* // my friend is helping me lie // down on her bed // I curl up into a foetal position // re-enter my mother's womb

acceptance

tonight, I am in her art studio // the night feels luminous // she takes out a pair of scissors // asks me // to sit // very still // *not too short, OK?* I murmur // I notice an eyelash // on her left cheek // I know it is not my place // to touch it // I listen to the crisp snip-snip // of silver on black // & I know I love her // this girl who is cutting my hair // her left hand cups my head // I want to say: *shame me through the night* // instead I watch my hair // slip down // like falling angels // to the sound // of our synchronised breath // she holds my steady gaze // in the mirror // & knows what I know

The Heart of the Matter

I could not bear this bewildering joy,
    awakening to a room without walls,
        by which I mean a room without eyes.

In a dream, I keep seeing her, my head-
    mistress. Though she is smiling, I am
        terribly afraid. *There is something you*

want to tell the world, she'd say,
    sipping a sencha tea, though she is not
        Japanese. *What?* I'd say. And she'd say:

That – pointing in the direction of
    my heart. And I'd say: *What?* And
        she'd say: *That, right there, that ache* –

The Window

Once in a lifetime, you will gesture
at an open window, tell the one who
detests the queerness in you that dead
daughters do not disappoint, free your
sore knees from inching towards a kind
of reprieve, declare yourself genderless as
hawk or sparrow: an encumbered body
let loose from its cage. You will refuse
your mother's rage, her spit, her tongue
heavy like the heaviest of stones. Her
anger is like the sun, which is like love,
which is the easiest thing, even on the
hardest of days. You will linger, knowing
that this standing before an open window
is what the living do: that they sometimes
reconsider at the slightest touch of grace.

母
親
的
故
事

what my mother (a poet) might say (1)

~~that she had scurvy as a child~~
~~that I don't understand hunger until I can describe what a drop of oil tastes like~~

that Mao wrote beautiful Chinese calligraphy

~~that she finds democracy to be the opiate of the masses~~
~~that I am a descendant of the Yellow Emperor~~

that Mao wrote beautiful Chinese calligraphy

~~that she dreams about seeing her father's heart in the doctor's fist~~
~~that I must only write about flowers~~

that Mao wrote beautiful Chinese calligraphy

~~that she showed her mother-in-law a blood-speckled sheet the morning after~~
~~that I shall love a man despite his ways~~

that Mao wrote beautiful Chinese calligraphy

~~that she wants to devour me back into herself~~
~~that I would be *ci sin* to love another woman~~

that Mao wrote beautiful Chinese calligraphy

~~that her neurons are a crumbling Great Wall~~
~~that I am a new earth arising from hierarchies of bone~~

that Mao wrote beautiful Chinese calligraphy

The Calligrapher

Try grasping a piece of wood
between your thumb, middle
& ring finger – as if the drip-
dripping of ink was a typhoon
you could play in. Loosen the
right wrist, scrape the weight
of too-much from brush/heart
across ink bowl; let its round
rim reassure. Sculpt the brush-
tip till shrill: sharp as papercut.
Let ink seep: a dot, a line, then
a mad dash to the last stroke till
interlocking arms form terraced
paddies bursting with meaning:
the character *fortune* made up of
the shirt on your back, the roof
over your head & the promise
of a stomach satisfied with rice.

When people ask why, reply:
my mother wished I would
write with the grace of those
ancient Chinese poets whose
tapestry now slips easily from
my ten-year-old tongue into a
diptych of shapes. Hour upon
hour, my wrist aches as the ink
dries to a crust. My eyes blink
back water, but this is precisely
the moment to continue. Once
more the fingers dip, slide, lift.
I am not a dancer, but this is a
dance. Hours spill into a pot of
tea leaves as my mother tells me:
See how Chinese characters are
sunflowers that seek out the eyes.
Seeds of ink unfurl suddenly from
your wrist, blooming into time –

母
親
的
故
事

RIPOSTE

At the Castro

for Orlando

the first time you stepped   into a gay bar
was the first time   you danced
not just a shuffle   or nodding to music
but limbs loosening   into whiplash
toes into tambourines   your tongue
whispering *oh my god*   strange hands
that love you so much   they start to steer
the shipwreck   of your body
into open waters   liquid light
flooding the room   that night
the girl who thought   she had to sit down
for the rest of her life   broke all the rules
became the wind   you drank till
you became sober   enough not to be
ashamed   a cathedral
of mouths   this is how heretics
become holy   by setting our own sighs
on fire   four years later
a hand   pulls a trigger
the music stops   how many
were shot before   their first kiss
what if you had been   stopped
by the bullet   into whose arms
would you have   surrendered
would you have known   the anguished
clutch   of your lover's breath
the way skin   is never an apology
but always   an act of faith

Names (1)

I am trying to talk about you without
mentioning your name, so I say: *We
went to see a film last night*, meaning

you and I, or *she treats me very well*,
as in, you love me, or *I'm going out
for curry tonight*, implying a candle-

lit dinner for two. It isn't always easy
keeping your name sheltered from my
mother's ears, but I try and try because

it keeps me from hearing that twist and
drop of her mouth, the way I try not to
imagine her standing next to the kitchen

sink at midnight, hungry for food or love,
though I know she will pilgrimage to that
sacred spot over and over, the way the owl

never forgets it can see its prey best in the
dark. I have now learnt to name my loves
sparingly. You know this, don't you, how

your name will never leave my mother's
lips? I want to apologise. You do know
how much I want you – us – to survive?

They Would Have All That

To sing the evening home, she prepares a pot
of lentil stew, her phone radiant with messages,
imagining her lover's steady hand gripping her
own phone to navigate towards some notion

of home, their flat a familiar place of worship,
their bodies growing close and moving apart
with the regularity of heartbeat, hot breath.
There the lover is, running to catch a bus,

wondering at her lover's motions throughout
the flat, how her feet must press on the floor
with each step, how the orchid must have
stretched itself a few millimetres overnight,

how the stew must be whispering on the stove
and the table laid for dinner. They are gentler
because they have memorised each other's fears
like daily prayer: how too much salt brings back

the years of loneliness, how a bath may be more
necessary than a rough kiss after a day's drought
of tenderness. They are gentler because they have
grown too knowledgeable to love any other way.

How have I hurt you? Such asking becomes routine,
almost like walking down the aisle of a supermarket
at evening, but it is what they do best. Beyond desire:
two clasped bodies holding the heart's ache at bay.

The Horse and the Monkey

I tell you that I am a horse, you
a monkey, fated by the Chinese
zodiac *to remain together as long*
as both partners practise the art
of compromise. The horse and
monkey can now be found
riding the wind at the fifth base
of Mount Fuji. We hold each other
as if our limbs were the mountain's
melting snow. All those days when
I believed the odds were bruised:
our zodiacs, my Chinese parents.
Your tofu skin against the butter
of mine. Moments before the plane
delivers us to ground, I beg amid
the turbulence – *please* – to Buddha,
even to the Lord who would never
grant me permission to love you.
I am bargaining with these whorls
of steel to keep going, in spite of
everything. At home, my mother
greets us both with these words:
I love monkeys. They are auspicious
creatures. In that moment, did you
realise that we were being blessed?

//

My mother lays the table with chopsticks & ceramic
spoons, expects you to fail at dinner. To the Chinese,

you & I are chopsticks: lovers with the same anatomies.
My mother tells you that *chopsticks* in Cantonese sounds

like *the swift arrival of sons.* My mother tongue rejoices
in its dumbness before you as expletives detonate: *[two*

women] [two men] [disgrace]. Tonight, I forget that I am
bilingual. I lose my voice in your mouth, kiss till blood

comes so *sorry* does not slip on an avalanche of syllables
into sorrow. I tell you that as long as we hold each other,

no apology will be enough. Tonight, I am dreaming again
of tomorrow: another chance to eat at the feast of the living

with chopsticks balanced across the bridges of our hands
as we imbibe each *yes,* spit out every *no* among scraps of

shell or bone. Father says: *Kids these days are not as tough*
as we used to be. So many suicides in one week. How many

times have you & I wondered about leaving our bodies
behind, the way many of us have already left? My friend's

sister loved a woman for ten years & each word she says
to her mother stings like a paper cut. Each word she does

not say burns like the lines she etches carefully into skin.
I have stopped believing that secrets are a beautiful way

to die. You came home with me for three hundred days –
to show my family that dinner together won't kill us all.

Notes Towards an Understanding

I

When you said: *Why didn't you warn me
about cultural differences?* I did not know
whether you meant my mother's face all
darkened like a curtain, or the vegetables.

II

When mother said: *The contours of her ears
are calamitous*, I momentarily reflected on
my own auditory shells, whether they too
played a part in my irrevocable queerness.

III

When father said: *I find language to be a
very difficult thing*, I wondered if he was
apologising for his silences, how he said
nothing when mother detonated my name.

IV

When I said: *I want to shout at all of you, but
in which language?* My mind was tuned to
two frequencies: mother's Cantonese rage,
your soothing English, inviting me to choose.

Versions from the Twenty-four Filial Exemplars

He Lay Down on Ice in Search of Carp

One of the strangest, this: *how a boy mistreated*
by his stepmother still tried to satisfy her cravings
for carp, sought out the frozen lake and thawed the ice with
bare skin, brought home two pregnant ones
for a pot of soup. At eight, I learnt this from my mother,
offered immediately to outdo this fabled son,
though there was no ice to be found across the city,
our temperate winters incapable of frost.
Years later, I wonder why my mother did not mention
hypothermia or the possibility of drowning, did not
invite me to wonder at the boy's lack
of self-respect, did not consider how his body
deserved its own morsel of warmth, how his fingers
should never have been bait.

He Fed the Mosquitoes with His Blood

Another begins with a sacrifice: *a boy too poor*
to afford mosquito nets offers his blood as nectar in his parents'
stead, as he sits on their bed on hot summer nights
to keep them safe from the unbearable scorch
of inflamed skin. I read this alone as a teenager,
my Chinese now oxidised as black tea, capable
of steeping in fabled warnings. Once more, I detect
how dispensable the child's body is, how right it is that he
suffers for an ideological wound, how his parents
might have slept fitfully that night, roused by their child's
cries as the mosquitoes encircled him, or perhaps
blinking back a tear while thinking how good
their boy is, how proper this bloody
business of proving one's love.

He Dressed Up to Amuse His Parents

No longer a boy, but an old man, dressed up
as a child to amuse his elderly parents, his fists
adorned with toys: a stick, a piece of polished stone.
This isn't the worst fable amongst the twenty-four,
but it makes me rage, because I am now
no longer in need of dolls, though my mother yearns
for my feet to shrink to the size of her
open palms, and for the rest
of me to follow. Some days I cannot be her
child again, although I pacify arguments
and tears with a playful voice
that pleases, if only to reassure her,
and to say that love
is patient, love is kind.

Written in a Historically White Space (1)

The reader stares at my 皮膚 and asks: why don't you write in 中文? I reply: 殖民主義 meant that I was brought up in your image. Let us be honest. Had I not learnt 英文 and come to your shores, you wouldn't be reading this poem at all. Did you think it was an accident that I learnt your 語言 for decades, until I knew it better than the 母語 I dreamt in? Is anything an accident these days? Dear reader, you are lucky to have been the centre of my 宇宙 for the past twenty years. One summer, a taxi driver in Shanghai asked me whether I was my lover's tour guide, declaring that she was from 大英帝國. How does that make me feel? Can you tell me what it is that I should do next?

This Grammatical Offer of Uniqueness is Untrue

I have never said *mother*
my entire life she speaks
Shanghainese and Mandarin
and Cantonese knows select
phrases in French or English
words like *sophisticated* multi-
syllabic she would pluck
them like sudden notes
from a warbler's throat
her magic sleight of hand
at a dinner party where one
of the guests is an elderly
white man (professorial)

when I say *mother* I mean
all those mothers I have
witnessed or envisioned
mothers of history and
mothers of our present
historical moment all
desperately trying to love
their children even those
the laws have deemed as
unworthy as washcloths
tumble-dried for the last
time dirt-ridden beyond help

Safe Space (II)

Wash your hands. Rub soap into foam
into lost hands. Focus on the running tap,
the way your hands momentarily disappear
and you feel safe again. The bathroom is a
place you can always rely on, in whatever
country, containing a door you are allowed
to lock. Lock the door, even though the flat
is empty and there are no mouths, no doors
that let the wild things through: wild love,
wild beauty, wild hurt, wild fear, all those
beasts and your inner voice whispering
these are the options: fight, flight or freeze

Rise and Shine

This morning your voice is a cleft wing
and the sky is echo. Your therapist says: *Avoid*
the foetal position because there will be too much blood
concentrated around the vital organs, by which

she means: *Try to sit up and greet the day anew.*
When air becomes a cage. When breathing
demands concentration: a striving
of muscle and sinew.

When syllables transmute into blabber, hiccup,
torrent leaking from every orifice on your devastated face.
Your voice is a river running deep underground.
Your lover asks for language, and you cannot give it.

Last night the faucet broke, and you cursed
the water for failing you. You have had enough
of water, that embryonic fluid that broke you
onto this patch of earth, screaming

and alone. Water reminds you of your mother's
grief, so you down three glasses and wish the ice caps
across the Arctic would flood the whole world.
Your lover's voice is so utterly ordinary

in its pain that you could almost empathise.
How did we survive? You whisper this
into her breasts, her hands smoothing your brow,
her voice in your ear like weather.

Long Distance

You are running on the rain-dark pavement through Sutton Park.
Where I am, sun. All the dehumidifiers are on in the house. No
fireplaces. Some seas are colder than others, some bodies warmer.
I am drinking Iron Buddha: leaves waiting for their time to blossom.
It is too spring here for my own good, too much green in the salad
bowl. Too many stories of salvation; earlier, blue beyond belief.
The moon is lying on its back in my dreams. What a smile looks
like. A toothbrush touches my lips. Asian steamed sea bass for
dinner with white rice. Victoria Harbour was named after your
queen. How many hearts in a deck of cards shuffled across two
continents? I am catching a plane again tonight, thinking about the
map on your neck.

Splitting

the poet does not understand everything
but being self-aware knows enough to say
splitting is a defence *mechanism* against
love and its absences
truth is a sky that burns dark
with all its hidden stars missed items
the poet has now singed so diligently
from the page: the time her mother
bought them a double bed
gifted her lover with a coral ring set in silver
a mother's talent for jewellery design
an artist's anguish how her mother
paid for plane tickets for two
invited them to stay and they did
the night she could no longer bear
their collective grief she wondered if any
of the joy would become apparent
in a future poem of hers

an ode to boundaries

hum of the radiator/rage
the art of being
supported &
surviving
alone

how healthy
i am, choosing
to betray her
to save the self
in formation

母親的故事

let them know

how you were handpicked
like the finest of pears
your childhood spent
in a diving pool

those clasped and taped wrists
hitting the water
the children stepping up
once more to the task
they cannot refuse

how you learnt to play
the piano then were chosen
for the local music conservatoire
but were replaced the day

the revolution arrived
your spot given
to *a worker's child*
how you left a decade later
for the colonised city

where even the tap water
was ceaselessly cold
and the citizens racist
your Shanghainese accent not fit

for those enamoured
of the Queen's English
how your writer's callus grew
for your pay cheque
cash sent to your siblings

and mother in Shanghai
all alive and trying to be well
you: a scriptwriter in a new dialect
expressions so easily crossed out

by a Cantonese hand
the red ink blotting the black

(Auto)biography

My detractors think they know me. Loud and always
too soft-hearted. The time I purchased fifty pairs of
frames from a sobbing woman whose eyewear shop
was closing down. The day I lost my father and cried
myself sick, until I thought I would never sing again,
though music was my only love during the revolution.
The time my daughter told me she was in love with a
woman and I lied and told her it would be OK. What
does three years of famine teach a person? Nothing.
Except that there is such a thing as perpetual hunger,
loss pounding on the windows like rain. Except that
my father loved me, and that he came back – as soon
as he could – in the swallowtail butterfly that fluttered
around the flat, in our pet Papillon, in my beloved child.

母親的故事

CORPS-À-CORPS

Flèche

History

At the age of thirteen, I wielded a blade because I had a firm grip, I was in love with Shakespeare, and the school team needed an épéeist. When my mother flew to Linz to watch me go 3–4 down against a former champion, she gripped the railing until her marriage ring was folded into flesh.

Strategy

You never duel against the same person, even if it is the same person. On the piste, once the blades are tilted upwards to signify respect, you recalibrate to thwart their every move. She was disarmed by my tears, a timeout to breathe through the yellowing bruise on my pale, yellow skin.

Footwork

Changing into school uniform felt like cross-dressing. I took my time: removing mask, then chest protector, lingering at the breeches. The day I learnt to lunge, I began to walk differently, saw distance as a kind of desire. Once, my blade's tip gently flicked her wrist: she said it was the perfect move.

Parry riposte

My greatest weakness: the riposte. In the changing room, the girl I was about to duel said I smelled of bitter gourd. We were practising the *flèche*. Inevitably, I collided with her, a blur of entangled blades. I glimpsed her wry expression through our masks' steel mesh: her gleaming, smiling lips.

Grip and point control

French or pistol grip: one offers stability, the other more room for surprise.
Before I came out to the world, I asked myself: *French or pistol grip?* Now,
you say: *You're a great lover.* Thank years of hard work on point control
– how two fingers manoeuvre the blade's tip – a flurry of sickle moons.

sorry

this is the scene of our domestic discord   you accusing me   of finding you
weak   when the waiter came over   with your pasta dish   & you apologised
for the trouble   I was upset at your vulnerability   all those times you
whispered *sorry*   your willingness to take any blame   whether deserved
or not   how it reminded me of my own eagerness to say   *yes, crucify*
me   how I learnt to apologise in my sleep   for this difficult torso   each
nightmare recalling   my struggle with daylight   for years it was this way
I could not bear my own shame   then we met &   I thought things would
change   but the truth is   I have carried your shame   & you have carried mine

Vigilance

I learnt to withhold my body / the way a dog lifts its sore paw / in mid-air / touching nothing / a life lived tenuously / my habitual position / is to remain very still / at all times / being queer was ultimately / a nurturing of vigilance / tip-toeing around words / as if each one could kill / listening for tiny triggers / that could cause my set face to blanch / my lover urges me out of the apartment / into a cruel world / though I am terribly afraid of mouths / capable of wielding language / like a winter threat / my torso shrinking into itself / for too long I have had to do these things / as when a great wind / pushes a small boat out to sea / before it is ready / I am the result / of my convictions / some of them weak / some of them ashamed / it was hard to feel bodily / fighting this labyrinth of longing / each time I take my therapist on merry-go-rounds / distract her from this deep-seated fear / this point of hurt

beauty

all the metaphors
have failed *the sea*
is infinitely breakable
my mother is raging
the way waves do
anger is a secondary
emotion a statement
from my therapist
who specialises in
honesty a rare trait
that calms me & she
is so beautiful I wish
I could summon all
the beauty in this
world ward off
any jagged feelings
I cannot stand the
faces of beautiful
women I feel a deep
need to protect any
plausible display of
happiness you see
my mother is fearful
of open windows
the abiding terror
of the world's light

song

a poet once said: *Getting what you want*
doesn't always make you happy
as we sat atop a bouldering block at the Castle
my fear of heights thinning the air
I am learning the world's inconsistencies
my lover wants me to be myself
which is both a brilliant and cruel prospect
sometimes my body wants to try cliff-diving
solo climb some unfathomable mountain
but my arms are weak as hand-pulled noodles
the poet who wrote *pain is indestructible*
praised me for not minding
when I tried three times
to solve a problem and failed
the blue holds glinting above our heads

Names (II)

everywhere / this same hall / of mirrors / the Panopticon / is inside me /
the men who keep watch / have my mother's eyes / I am the prodigal son
my grandmother wanted / but never got / I am the wayward daughter /
my mother never deserved / so when I am greeted with / *Sir* / *Sir* / *Sir* / on
the streets / of London / in the cafe / of the British Library / I blame myself
/ blame the clothes I chose / thought camouflage / was a fashion label /
I could hide behind / can hear my mother's voice / *it's your fault* / *they've*
mistaken you / *for a boy* / but I love my riot of black spikes / love these
shoes / I allow myself to wear / in a country far / from home / so when
I am met / at the threshold / of each bathroom / with the frightened jerk
of a woman / pushing the door open / I say nothing / insist on my body's
relevance to conditional spaces / twice I say: / *this is the women's bathroom*
/ hoping that my voice / would do the trick / their confusion becomes mine /
the way my name has become mine / through the years of being summoned
/ the way a dog / might be taught / how to fetch a fallen branch / heavy now
in the soft mouth / today I run again / through a sea of eyes / to find myself
redeemed / by a child's voice / when she said my name / it was spoken /
with utter kindness / the kind of tone / only children are capable of / I felt
as if her voice was a sign / for me to finally relinquish / my own cruelty /
towards myself / how strange to think / I've been looking everywhere / for
forgiveness / and all it takes is an eight-year-old / to gently speak / my name

Wish

I would like to live like the trees
my lover often says *look up!*
as she admires a canopy of green
her tree-like behaviour astounds me
if you looked within me now, you'd see
that my languages are like roots
gnarled in soil, one and indivisible
except the world divides me endlessly
some days I dare not look at the trees
they are such hopeful creatures
if the legislators of our world
looked to their trees for guidance
would they reconsider everything?
lately I've been trying to write
a poem that might birth a tree
a genuine acceptance of the self
continues to elude me

Dragon Hill Spa

Seoul, South Korea

In memory of all 'comfort women'

It is the year 20—, but you know
how women tame their bodies

into bones, dig their own graves
in daylight. Here, in a hot bath

of rainbows, the bodies let themselves
go, the water holds them up to the light,

the lips murmur a prayer to skin. Here,
the only hands that touch their wrists

are their own. Here is no man's land.
Here, the names of soldiers, heavy-

handed, are forgotten. Here, no one
takes what they want from the women

whose gods are freely chosen,
whose bones are theirs to bury.

Written in a Historically White Space (II)

I grew up in a city where parks once displayed
this sign in my mother tongue: CHINESE and
DOGS NOT ALLOWED. We were creatures
with knees kissing colonial ground. That was
history; this act of mutual regard, the present.
We are stereotypes of yellow because the way
out is always through the flutter of your white
eyelids. Skin is the distinguishing factor of this
age in which I, a diligent student of English
literature, can be presumed at a glance to
belong behind the till, the man who had just
seen the same film I had seen turning to me to
ask: *Are you selling tickets for the new releases?*
Can you see how much effort it takes to face
a white mouth with so much to (dis-)prove?
Every day I try to love the world, until my
joints inflame, ache, resenting me for it.

The Importance of Tea

When your aunt arrived, she asked for
normal tea, which, to my untrained ears,
sounded a bit like *normality*. In Hong
Kong, normal tea is green, or white, or
red. It took my mind several moments
to move from green to white to red to
land on black. Your aunt was flexible:
Any Assam, Darjeeling or Earl Grey?
We only had matcha, some loose-leaf
Iron Buddha in the cupboard, no milk.
Your aunt looked at you as if you'd
failed at being British, me as if I'd failed
to properly assimilate. Afterwards, you
said I was projecting onto your aunt the
fears I harboured. No matter how many
years I've spent in this country, how
I interpret normal tea, what is normal
to me. You are learning Mandarin
Chinese. I see how the characters are
split for you: signifier and signified
refuse to conjoin. That's what happened
when your aunt asked for the *normal
tea*. Days later, when a waiter brought
us white sugar for our Oolong tea at
a cafe, I caught your gaze. We laughed
and left the sachets unopened.

speaking in tongues

mother says: *fan lei*   分離
poet says: *behave*
mother says: *seng sin*   聲線
poet says: *moonbeam*
mother says: *separation of voice*
poet says: *behave, moonbeam*
mother says: *the way you ask the moon*
to behave is transgressive, not Chinese
poet says: *my voice is a splinter*

tin hei   天氣
these days
I can only speak about the weather
with a tongue splitting
spitting monosyllabic blue or grey
but did you know
I've discovered a secret
that half of my words
have been kept like a key
under a plant
which my mother waters daily
and is something that grows
those beautiful ghosts
they seem to say:
jing dak nei   認得你

One Breath

I have been hearing it everywhere these days, that sudden song-burst from the throats of the still-too-young, their world too tragic for silence, leaving them no choice but to grip their mothers' arms as if touch were breath, as if no sorrow could bear this moment when a cry becomes the world, the song that might cost them their lives unravelling from their throats – a spool of flung thread rising, a blown-bubble till it bursts, releasing its fury into gasps, yawps, howls – all the sounds a body makes when it becomes its own instrument, rehearsing the songs it has learnt across the centuries, forgetting how young it still is, how long moss takes to green, how much ripening awaits.

Safe Space (III)

where the logic of hips isn't a stranglehold to the heart

where you kiss my eyelid with the windows flung open

where a sudden light in the corridor calms like a cure

where no one wrings the air in a drawn-out expletive

where I am naked in the shadow of evening & unafraid

an eternal &

nothing but the enlightened land   soil loosening into surf   sinking softly
the weight of hours   every second   symphonic   ocean is never elsewhere

always here   in the eternal stillness   of depths   ripples eyeing the shore
wings arching origami   out of air   you are there   a shape I have come to

know so well   your head   is a compass   your arms   slipping between
the ocean's breath   I am ready to hold   a body of sun   kiss it nine times

goodnight   time is elsewhere   as silence deafens into sound   we are holding
each other   amid the night's falling   all the stars   have plunged to earth

a glistening pier   *look* I say to you   *listen watch*   how we can make it through
another day   on this shore   of lifetimes   we'll have this ocean   an eternal &

母
親
的
故
事

Tea Ceremony

There are days when I pretend
to understand my mother's grief,

as I coax her into sitting at the table
for a tea ceremony, so she might

linger on the rush of green into
glass, how the scent of leaf

dissolves both past and future
in one gulp. We drink in a serene

silence, my mother smiles a smile
that breaks my breath into laughter.

She is radiant now, lost in the kettle's
repetitive chant, her gaze fixed on

the dance of fingers between utensils.
I love my mother's joy, her reprieve

from the sorrow she adorns with
designer clothing. Some nights,

I tell her: *Go to bed*. She says: *I can't.*
Can you stay? As a child, I dreaded

her desperate need, my hand resting
on her forehead, unable to let go.

Even now, with Winnicott and Klein
as bedside reading, I can only invite her

to the table: *Look, Mother, your hands
are beautiful. Look, our tea is ready.*

what my mother (a poet) might say (II)

be a river she might say
  be the water that flows
    over & under & along

so you will never hurt from
  sharp things be the eyes
    that glow be the body

whose scent & sound attract
  all the colours of the night
    be the rainbow that leaps

into that cleansed dome
  of sky after storms erupt
    from the breasts of millions

be the tree that praises
  even when the cacophony
    of tractors drown out its hymns

be the roots that seep
  through stone be the echo
    of your blood song of your bones

母親的故事

Notes

PARRY: a fencing blade-work move used to deflect or block an incoming attack.

RIPOSTE: an offensive fencing technique which is used with the intent of hitting one's opponent, usually after one 'parries' an attack, hence the use of 'parry riposte' in fencing parlance.

CORPS-À-CORPS: used in fencing parlance to describe two fencers coming into physical contact with one another.

'Dress' references Jean-Paul Sartre's phrase 'Hell is other people' from his play *No Exit*.

'The Calligrapher' visually evokes two long scrolls of rice paper (usually laid out side by side) on which Chinese calligraphy is typically written. The 'shang lian' (上聯) or 'upper phrase' usually requires a corresponding 'xia lian' (下聯) or 'lower phrase'.

'The Twenty-four Filial Exemplars' is a Confucian text on filial piety written during the Yuan Dynasty (1260–1368) which has been used as a classic example of how children should honour their parents.

'Splitting' refers to the psychoanalytic theory of 'splitting', first coined by the Scottish psychoanalyst Ronald Fairbairn, who is widely known for his theory of object relations.

'speaking in tongues' uses select lyrics from Faye Wong's 1990s Cantonese pop song 'Promise' (約定).

'an eternal &': the line 'kiss it nine times goodnight' plays on one of the many homophones of the word 'nine' (九) in both Mandarin Chinese and Cantonese; in this case: 'eternal' (久).

Acknowledgements

Grateful acknowledgements are made to the following publications, in which some of my poems first appeared: *Poetry Review*, *Poetry London*, *PN Review*, *White Review*, *Ambit*, *Wasafiri*, *London Magazine*, *English: Journal of the English Association*, *The Rialto*, *Magma*, *The Scores*, *Callaloo*, *Asian American Writers' Workshop*, *Bare Fiction*, *Close: TinyLetter*, *Tongue* and *Carcanet New Poetries VII*.

Thanks are due to the following writers for their poetry and poetics, which are often directly present in my work: James Baldwin, Emily Berry, Vahni Capildeo, Hélène Cixous, Michael Cunningham, Édouard Glissant, Marie Howe, Sarah Howe, Saeed Jones, Kei Miller, Claudia Rankine, Adrienne Rich, Denise Riley and Ocean Vuong.

I am profoundly grateful to my poetry mentors for their generous support. My deepest thanks to Jo Shapcott for her guidance during the MA and PhD at Royal Holloway and beyond. Profound thanks to Emily Berry and Sarah Howe for their continual inspiration, advice and friendship. Thank you to Alan Buckley for his editorial wisdom, and to Katrina Naomi for her mentorship through the Poetry Society's Anne Born Prize.

Heartfelt thanks to Matthew Hollis and Lavinia Singer for their patience, care and astute editorial guidance, and to my literary agent, Emma Paterson, for believing in and championing my work. I am also thankful to Sandeep Parmar and Sarah Howe for their pioneering work to cultivate a new generation of BAME critics through the Ledbury Poetry Critics programme.

This book is lovingly dedicated to my parents, who have unconditionally nurtured and supported my love of the written word; and to my partner, Jo, whose presence in my life has made this book – and everything else – possible.

FLÈCHE